Ava's
WISH

written by Alisha Prather and Sadie Wilks
illustrated by Tagan Mire

Ava had a simple wish.

You see, Ava was a little girl
who loved people,
and her greatest wish was to help others.

Ava loved to help her mom fix their
favorite snack, cheese and chips.
And she loved to share her snacks with
someone who was sick or feeling sad.

Ava loved playing school with her sisters
and she dreamed of becoming a teacher,
because teachers help people learn
so many things.

Ava wanted to help as many people as she could.
Helping others made her happy,
and she loved giving people something
they really needed.

Some people needed Ava's time.
She loved helping her mom clean
windows at home.

Some people needed Ava's talents.
She enjoyed drawing and sharing her
pictures with friends to make their days brighter.

Some people needed Ava's smile.
Her grandma always made Ava smile when she let
her help cook macaroni for family dinners.

She once brought her neighbors a dozen of newly-dyed Easter eggs because she thought they were hungry.

She knew that her neighbors needed the food more than the Easter Bunny did!

No matter what people needed, large or little, Ava gave them her best.

All she wanted in return was their smile. Ava was thankful for every chance she had to help others.

One day, Ava was hurt and could not get better, so she went to heaven to be with God.

God saw how much she loved helping people when she was on Earth, so he asked her to be one of His Helper angels.

Helper angels live in Heaven
and help people on Earth.

Helper angels like Ava are rare and very special.
They give of themselves to help others in need.

Ava loves God and she loves helping people.
She especially loves being a Helper angel.

Have you seen Helper angels at work around you?

Helper angels draw rainbows after it rains,

and they make fluffy clouds into funny shapes in the sky.

They send butterflies to friends and family members who need to see something beautiful.

Helper angels ask birds to sing joyful tunes.

Ever since she went to heaven,
Ava's family misses her every day.
But they see her work around them
and know that Ava's wish to help
others comes true anytime someone
smiles or is comforted by the work
of a Helper angel.

They see Ava's wish come true when a child
is able to run and play again because
she gave them a special part from her heart.

They see Ava's wish come true when another child is able to live a healthier life because she gave them one of her kidneys or a part of her liver.

Ava's greatest wish on Earth was to help others. When she went to Heaven, God granted her wish.
And that makes all who knew her smile.

AVA GRACE BRANSTETTER

On May 26, 2016, just one day after graduating from kindergarten, my sweet 6 year old, Ava Grace, suffered a catastrophic spinal cord injury in a car wreck. As a result of her spinal cord injury, she then suffered brain death. I made the choice to donate Ava's organs so that others could receive the gift of life through her death and so that her death would not be in vain – something positive could come from the worst pain of our lives. As a mother, trying to explain brain death to Ava's twin sister (Olivia, 6) and big sister (Madeline, 9) was incredibly difficult and challenging. My hope is that this book will help explain organ donation to other children – siblings, cousins, friends, classmates, etc. – who are also facing this unimaginable pain and loss. My hope is also that this book will help increase organ donation awareness. Last, but not least, this book was written to honor Ava Grace who became a hero at 6 years old. Ava saved the lives of 4 people who would not be here today without Ava's donations.
– Emily, Ava Grace's Mother

For information on organ, tissue and eye donation
and stories like Ava's, please visit LOPA.org.

As the organ procurement
organization for Louisiana, LOPA
helps save lives, restore health and
enhance medical care through
organ and tissue donation. The
agency is a non-profit that services
Louisiana's diverse community
by supporting families through
tragic loss, during the donation
process, and along their grief
journey. LOPA team members
are passionate about sharing the
impact of donation and educating
professionals and the community.

*On LOPA.org, click on the
'Community Education' tab for
access to educational materials
for all ages.

The Gifted Life podcast offers
entertaining and informative
conversations about organ, tissue
and eye donation & transplantation.
Our goal is to raise awareness about
the need for these life saving gifts.
Share your inspiring stories with us
at info@TheGiftedLife.org.

TheGiftedLife.org

The LOPA Foundation is designed
as a 501(c)3 charitable and tax
exempt organization dedicated to
enhancing LOPA's capacity in the
areas of education, outreach and
family services.

LOPAFoundation.org

Ava's ART

ALL ABOUT MY MOM

1. My mom is really good at **making cupcakes.**

2. My favorite thing to do with my mom is **to go shopping.**

3. I think my mom is pretty when she wears **pretty things.**

4. It makes my mom happy when I **smile.**

5. I know my mom loves me because **Jesus made us.**

I am thankful for my mom!
HAPPY MOTHER'S DAY

Love,

I like the bech.
I like to swim noah
I pesa.

Let's JOURNAL

Parents and caregivers are encouraged to use our heroes' stories to discuss organ, tissue and eye donation with children, as well as other important concepts such as sharing and helping others.

Tell us about your hero ...

_____

_____

_____

_____

_____

_____

_____

_____

_____

_____

_____

Let's DRAW

Show us your hero ...

The Gifted Life Series: Ava's Wish

The Gifted Life series is published by the Louisiana Organ Procurement Agency (LOPA) to share heroic stories of organ, tissue and eye donors and their families, as well as the recipients of their gifts. It is an extension of The Gifted Life podcast also produced by LOPA (TheGiftedLife.org). *Ava's Wish* is the inaugural book in this series.

Acknowledgements and thanks:
Ava Grace Branstetter's family
Lori Steele, LOPA Community Educator, Media Specialist
    and The Gifted Life Podcast co-host
Samantha Miller, LOPA Quality Assurance, Safety and Health Administrator

All those who donated their time, talent and services to this special project:
Alisha Prather and Sadie Wilks
Tagan Mire
Elizabeth Perry